Tell Me
about Yourself

Tell Me about Yourself

How to Interview Anyone from Your Friends to Famous People

by D.L. Mabery

Lerner Publications Company   Minneapolis

LIBRARY OF CONGRESS CATALOGING IN PUBLICATION DATA

Mabery, D. L.
   Tell me about yourself.

   Summary: Describes how to arrange, prepare for, and
conduct an interview, with examples and suggestions of
interview opportunities in school and various careers.
      1. Interviewing (Journalism)—Juvenile literature.
[1. Interviewing (Journalism)] I. Title
PN4784.I6M27 1985   070.4'3   85-7001
ISBN 0-8225-1604-7 (lib. bdg.)

Manufactured in the United States of America

   2   3   4   5   6   7   8   9   10   94   93

To Jana Godfrey

CONTENTS

CONTENTS

The Interview 36

Breaking the Ice
Getting Down to Business
When Things Go Wrong

After the Interview 46

Transcribing Your Notes
Using the Information
Getting More Information
Keeping Your Notes
Saying Thanks

It's Your Turn! 60

Where to Begin
School Reports
School Newspaper
Practice for Celebrity Interviews
Career Opportunities
Other Rewards

Glossary of Terms 67

WHAT IS
AN INTERVIEW?

Heavyweight boxer Evander Holyfield is talking with Arsenio Hall, the host of the television talk-show that bears his name, "The Arsenio Hall Show." Both men are sitting on a couch facing the cameras, engaged in a conversation, looking relaxed. They are discussing Holyfield's experiences as a boxer, and the publicity that comes to someone who is involved in the sport.

Arsenio Hall asks his guest to clarify a recent rumor suggesting that Holyfield is involved with drugs. "[Boxing promoter] Bob Aram said something about you and steroids? It's a serious issue ....You were down at a school this morning talking to kids and I know that must be a problem when someone tells a lie like that on you."

"I don't take any steroids," Holyfield begins to explain, "and any time someone does that for any reason—slanders somebody—especially when kids look up to you, they start thinking that the only way you can compete is by taking steroids. That takes away from my performance...."

Holyfield elaborates on how he has tried to emphasize the importance of honest success, especially because he has become a role model for so many young children.

Each night "The Arsenio Hall Show" features celebrity guests on the program. The guests sit on a stage, on a couch next to the host, where they answer questions and talk about themselves.

Arsenio Hall moves the conversation away from the boxer's public life and inquires about Holyfield's family: "Why does your mom call you Chubby?"

"It's something I've asked her, because I was short, but I wasn't fat—she named me after her girlfriend," Holyfield ruefully explains. It seems that this is an embarrassing fact he wants to forget, but no one will let him: ". . . it wasn't too cool, but it stuck with me."

Unbelieving, the host asks, "And she still calls you Chubby?"

Holyfield grins and shyly replies, "I'm still her little baby!"

The conversation between Evander Holyfield and Arsenio Hall is known as an **interview**. An interview is a meeting in which one person obtains information ·from another person. In the above example, a talk-show host is obtaining information from a well-known athlete. In another kind of interview, an employer obtains information from someone applying for a job.

Most **journalists**, those people who write for newspapers or narrate news stories on television or radio, gather much of the information they pass on to you through interviewing people. There are several ways of conducting interviews, just as there are a variety of uses for the information that is collected. The two most common kinds of interviews are the **fact-finding interview** and the **informational interview**.

The Fact-Finding Interview

The fact-finding interview is used when a reporter needs specific information about a given subject. For example, let's say that a reporter is writing a story about a new convention center in the downtown area. The reporter knows that the convention center will also include a theater. To finish the story, the reporter needs to know how much it will cost to build the theater and how many people it will hold.

How will the reporter obtain this information? He or she can call the city planning committee and arrange a meeting with the person most likely to know the answers to the reporter's questions. In a few short minutes, the reporter can ask specific questions and get the facts needed to finish the news story. This kind of interview can usually be conducted over the telephone and does not even require that the two people meet each other.

The Informational Interview

The informational interview is the kind most people think of when they hear the word "interview." As in the fact-finding interview, the reporter requires information. But unlike the fact-finding interview, the reporter is not seeking a specific answer. Rather, she or he wishes to obtain general knowledge about a person or particular event. Most often it is a famous person being interviewed—a singer or actor, for instance—and the reporter wants biographical details for an article. Perhaps the interview will concentrate on the star's latest project, such as a film or a record. The interview with Evander Holyfield on "The Arsenio Hall Show" is an example of an informational interview.

The informational interview is conversational in structure. It could even be compared to two friends who haven't seen each other for a while, and who are discussing what they have done since they last met. The only real difference, of course, is that the reporter doesn't talk about her or himself. While the informational interview is more relaxed in nature than the fact-finding interview, it must also be structured so that the reporter can learn as much as possible during the time allotted for the interview.

ARRANGING
AN INTERVIEW

Before you can arrange an interview, you must first decide what kind of interview you want to do and who you want to interview. These two decisions go hand-in-hand.

Deciding Who to Interview

For a good interview, the reporter must find a person who possesses a significant amount of knowledge about the subject he or she is researching—or someone with an interesting story to tell. If you need to check facts, you will conduct a fact-finding interview. If you want to write a longer story, you will probably need to do one or more informational interviews.

How will you decide who to interview for a story? If you are preparing a story on race-car driving, for example, you wouldn't interview your next-door neighbor—unless, of course, that neighbor is the world-famous driver Parnelli Jones or some other authority on the subject.

On the other hand, you might want to interview the same neighbor if you are writing a story about neighborhood parks.

For a fact-finding interview, you must decide ahead of time what information you are seeking and who might be the most qualified person to supply you with the information. It is quite possible that you already know of a person who is an expert on the subject. In a case like this, the problem would not be *who* to interview, but whether that person has time to meet with you.

Most of the time, the questions can be answered in a quick phone call, particularly if the reporter only needs one or two answers. If the person doesn't have the necessary few minutes free or if the interview is more involved than that, you and the other person can agree on a time when you should call back or meet in person.

Choosing a subject for an informational interview is not as easy. If you are writing a story on juggling, you might want to conduct informational interviews with one or more jugglers to find out how long they have been juggling, where they learned to juggle, and any other pertinent information. Informational interviews take more time and must be scheduled in advance. Although they can be conducted over the phone, it is always better if you are able to conduct an informational interview in person.

Scheduling the Interview

When you have determined what kind of interview to conduct and whom you would like to interview, you can then proceed to schedule the interview.

When you call someone for a fact-finding interview, glance at your questions first and try to judge how much time they will take to answer. Then be sure to mention to the person that you will only need five (or ten) minutes of his or her time.

Gathering adequate material in an informational interview can take up to an hour, if the person being interviewed can afford that much time. Interviewing time is usually determined by how much time the person has available for the meeting. Most of the time you will have to adjust your own schedule around the other person's in order to get the interview.

Sometimes one phone call is all it takes to secure an interview. Some people are much harder to reach than others, so be prepared to have to call back several times just to reach the person. You may have to call back again after the person has had time to consult his or her schedule.

Securing an Interview with Someone Famous

Obtaining permission to interview a famous

person can be even more complicated. Rarely can a reporter dial a number and be immediately connected with a celebrity. The rich and famous are extremely busy, and their schedules are usually planned well in advance. If, for instance, a reporter in Buffalo, New York, wishes to interview Paula Abdul when she comes to Buffalo on tour, the reporter will probably have to schedule the interview several weeks before the concert date.

Most celebrities employ a person to handle their schedules. This person, known as a **press agent**, makes arrangements for TV and news reporters to interview the stars. A reporter trying to get an interview with a well-known singer, actor, or actress will probably have to schedule the appointment with the press agent. The press agent will check the celebrity's schedule and tell the reporter when the interview can take place. Both patience and determination are required when a reporter sets out to get an interview with someone famous.

My experience in securing an appointment with Bette Midler provides a good example. I had heard that Ms. Midler was to perform several concerts in Minneapolis, where I work, in two months' time. I called the concert promoter, who gave me the name and phone number of Ms. Midler's press agent in Los Angeles. I phoned the agent, identified myself, and inquired about the possibility of interviewing the star over the telephone prior to the concert dates. The paper I worked for wanted to print the interview a few days before Ms. Midler's concert appearance.

The agent informed me that Ms. Midler was not granting any interviews during her concert tour. However, her plans included a return trip to Minneapolis three months later to publicize a book she had written. "There is the possibility that you could interview Bette at that time," he told me.

Before ending my phone conversation with the press agent, I got his mailing address and told him that I would send him copies of interviews I had written up. This way, the agent would have the opportunity to see samples of my work. Not only would this let him see my writing style, but it was also a way to remind the agent of my name before we spoke again. I was certain the agent would receive numerous requests from other reporters to interview Ms. Midler, and I wanted to insure being considered when the agent began making the appointments.

About six weeks before Ms. Midler was to return to Minneapolis to publicize the book, I again called the press agent and reminded him of our previous conversation. The agent remembered my name and even commented on the articles I had sent. No interviews had been finalized yet, he said, but he would keep me in mind. About two weeks later, the agent called me. He told me that I would have the opportunity to talk with Ms. Midler in person and that the time and place of the interview would be finalized after Ms. Midler had arrived in Minneapolis.

Getting this interview was the result of persistence and a lot of phone calls. I started the process five months before the interview actually took place. And in fact, I was the only reporter in Minneapolis who was granted an interview with Ms. Midler during the book tour.

PREPARING FOR THE INTERVIEW

You might think that once you have scheduled an interview, you can sit back and relax until it is time for it to take place. Wrong! You must *prepare* for the interview.

Doing Proper Research

Probably the single most important step you can take to prepare for a successful interview is to do research on your topic. If you are interviewing someone who is an expert on that topic, you should know as much as you can about the topic so that the person will not have to spend too much time explaining it to you.

Experienced reporters know that their job at the interview is to collect the greatest amount of information in the smallest amount of time. Frequently some of the information a reporter might wish to obtain in the interview can be found before the interview even takes place. A reporter doesn't want to waste any time getting answers she or he could learn by doing some research.

The same rule holds true if you are interviewing a famous person. Because famous people are asked the same questions over and over, they quickly become bored with interviews. But the answers to those typical questions usually find their way into print in newspapers and magazines, and you can read the answers before you even go to the interview. Before you meet with a well-known personality, go to the library and find out as much as you can about the person you are going to interview.

One of the most useful tools you will find at the library is the *Reader's Guide to Periodical Literature*. This set of reference books is a comprehensive list of articles printed in magazines. The guide is divided into volumes according to time period, such as July–December 1992. Within each volume, magazine articles are listed according to topic. If you were looking for information about Jodie Foster, who starred in "The Silence of the Lambs," you would look up her name in the book. If you wanted recent information, you would begin with the most recent volume and progress back through the years.

This kind of research also pays off in another way. As you read, you will probably think of new questions that have not been answered in previous articles. You can then use the valuable interview time to ask these questions.

The first major interview I ever conducted was with the author Truman Capote. Mr. Capote was famous for having written a number of books, including *Breakfast at Tiffany's* and *In Cold Blood,* which were made into movies. This information was all I knew about the author at the time I scheduled the interview, and I needed to know much more. By reading articles about Mr. Capote in various magazines in the library, I found out that he was working on two different books at the time. I also learned that he grew up in the South and was raised by an aunt. This knowledge helped me understand the author better and gave me ideas for things to talk about during the interview.

Research can also keep a reporter out of embarrassing situations. I learned this the hard way. When I was scheduled to interview Steve Goodman, I wrote up my list of questions without knowing what the singer had worked on during the past couple of years. I knew only that Steve Goodman was the man who wrote the song called "The City of New Orleans" and other folk songs that told a story.

During the interview, Mr. Goodman said that he liked to perform concerts. He believed that his storytelling songs were easier for people to understand when performed onstage. When he recorded an album in the studio without an audience, he felt that much of the magic of his performance was lost.

Since Mr. Goodman enjoyed performing concerts so much, I asked if he had considered recording a concert album.

Mr. Goodman paused for a moment, then said ruefully, "I guess you haven't heard my last album. It was recorded live, in concert." While it may have been difficult for me to have heard *all* of his albums prior to the interview, I would have known of the live album had I done even basic research. Instead, I gave the singer the impression that I wasn't interested enough in him to find out. As a result, Mr. Goodman immediately became more distant as he responded to the rest of my questions. I could tell that he wanted to complete the interview as quickly as he could.

On the other hand, having done proper research paid off handsomely when I interviewed puppeteer Wayland Flowers. With a puppet named Madame, Wayland Flowers appeared regularly on the television programs "Hollywood Squares" and "Solid Gold." During my research I discovered that Mr. Flowers was planning a Broadway show that would feature his puppet Madame. I also learned that the man was raised in a religious household. This was an interesting point, because the puppet Madame was notorious for her dirty jokes.

During the interview I asked about the Broadway show. I also asked the puppeteer what his family thought about his raunchy act. He responded openly, and we talked for quite some time about how the success he enjoyed made it easier for his family to accept the puppet's dirty jokes. When the interview was completed, Mr. Flowers thanked me for a good interview, and said, "You managed to ask questions I haven't been asked before. That is nice."

While doing your research, questions will come to mind that you will want to ask during the interview. At this time, you should begin compiling your list of questions. Once you have thought out all the questions, you should then go through the list and organize them in the order in which you intend to ask them. During the interview, of course, you may think of new questions and can jot them down on your list.

Preparing Your List of Questions

Take a few minutes to think about your topic. After your research, what do you know about the subject? What would you *like* to know?

The list of questions you carry into the interview must be carefully thought out. Each question should lead logically into the next one. To jump from one topic to another without some sort of progression is confusing and unsettling. To avoid this, you must decide which question to ask first, which one to ask next, and so on. Continue one line of questioning until you feel you have a complete answer and then change directions.

There are also situations in which a reporter must ask a question that someone might not want to answer. This happens frequently with reporters who are interviewing politicians or police officers. For example, let's say that a reporter has an interview with the chief of police the day after two policemen were killed while making an arrest. The reason the men were killed is unclear, and the reporter wants to find the answer. Because the chief of police hasn't issued a statement about the killings, there is a good possibility that he or she won't want to talk about the subject at the time of the interview.

If the very first question the reporter asks the police chief is "Why were the men killed last night?" the reporter may not get too far. The police chief might refuse to answer and be suspicious and uncooperative during the rest of the interview. He or she might decide to terminate the interview right away, and the reporter would have to leave the interview without any information whatsoever. If, however, the reporter drew up a list of questions with neutral subjects at the beginning of the interview and saved the touchy question for last, then he or she could at least leave the interview with some usable information.

Knowing Your Directions

An equally important part of preparing for an interview is knowing how to get to the site of your interview and making sure you will be there on time. When you have arranged to meet someone in a place you've never been before, be sure you have the proper directions.

I once caused an interview with a book author to be 45 minutes late because I was sitting in the wrong hotel lobby. We had agreed to meet in the author's hotel lobby before going to lunch. I got the directions confused and went to a hotel across town from where we were supposed to meet. After I waited a half hour without seeing the author, I figured something must be wrong. I called back to my office to see if he had cancelled the appointment only to be informed that I was waiting at the wrong hotel.

Immediately I phoned the author and explained what had happened. Fortunately for me, the author had no other appointments that day and he still had time to see me. I missed lunch, of course, but that was a small price to pay for my mistake. We did have coffee in his hotel room and I acquired my interview.

Looking the Part

Preparations for an interview should also extend to your personal appearance. First impressions can make or break an interview. A reporter with a sloppy personal appearance can give the person being interviewed the wrong impression before the interview has even started.

If you look disorganized and haphazard, the person you interview may think that your work is that way too. Instead, you must convey a professional image. You are a responsible journalist, concerned with the tasks of recording information accurately and using it wisely.

AN INTERVIEWER'S MATERIALS

Just as a camper must prepare for a trip by gathering camping gear and stowing it in the trunk of the car, a reporter must bring a number of items to the interview. The bare essentials include a notepad and at least two pens. Many interviewers also use a tape recorder and some even bring a camera to the interview.

Reporter's Notebook

All reporters take notes. This enables them to reconstruct their thoughts hours later while writing the story. When going to an interview, you should always carry a pad of paper and more than one pen, in case the first pen runs out of ink. Ballpoint pens are best because they won't smudge or wash away. Notes taken with felt-tipped pens can disappear if water gets on the pages. More than once my reporter's notebook has been caught in the rain with me. The pages got wet, but my notes were intact.

Even if you are using a tape recorder to tape the interview, you will still need your notebook to write down new questions that pop into your head during the interview. A notebook is also handy for recording your observations about the person you are interviewing and possibly even the setting in which you are meeting.

To communicate a fuller sense of the person you are going to write about, it is a good idea to note personal details like clothing and mannerisms. During my interview with Bette Midler, I made notes about the clothing she wore and how her hair was styled. I even noted the fact that she drank bottled water. These details, when added to the final story, gave Bette Midler's personality another dimension that would not have been possible had the article only contained the information she gave me.

Tape Recorder

Most reporters record long interviews on a tape recorder to insure that every word their subject says will be remembered accurately. Unless a reporter knows shorthand, it is next to impossible to write down everything another person is saying without missing words or sentences.

To understand how slow and difficult note-taking can be, try this exercise some time. One evening when your parents are talking, grab a pad and a pen and start writing down everything they say to one another. Try to get every word as it is spoken. Don't ask them to stop talking when you fall behind. You'll be amazed at how quickly conversation progresses and how slow the note-taking process is.

Tape recorders are also useful for another reason: they allow reporters to maintain eye-to-eye contact with their subjects. Imagine how you would feel if you were being interviewed and were forced to talk to the top of the reporter's head while he or she was looking down taking notes. You might begin to wonder if the reporter was actually listening to you. If you are not using a tape recorder, try to look up from your notepad frequently—it will reassure the other person that you are interested in what he or she is saying.

The reporter who consistently looks down at a notepad also misses another form of communication: **body language**. How someone sits, how frequently he or she smiles or shifts in the chair, and other subtle movements tell a reporter something beyond the words being spoken. These movements offer clues as to what kinds of questions might be most welcome.

Quite often, the person you are interviewing will say something that you didn't anticipate while compiling your list of questions. In normal conversation, you would recognize this conversation cue and ask a new question. If you are free from the task of note-taking, it will be that much easier to follow the flow of conversation.

For these reasons, a tape recorder can be your best friend in an interview situation. You simply turn on the machine and start talking. Unfortunately, if the batteries fail or the tape breaks, the tape recorder can also become your worst enemy.

You should always be prepared for these situations, because they happen more often than you would think. If you are planning to rely on a tape recorder during an interview, take extra batteries and extra tapes with you. Right before your interview, check the recorder to be sure it is working.

Most tape recorders come with an electrical cord that plugs into a wall socket, which prevents you from having to count on the batteries at all. But there may not be an outlet where you are conducting the interview, or the outlet may not be convenient. In some cases, such as an outdoor interview, you will know this ahead of time. But in other cases, you will have no way of knowing, so you must be prepared for either situation. If you have counted on using electricity where there is none and haven't bothered to replace the dead batteries in your machine, it will be useless.

You will get the information you came for if you

know from the beginning of the interview that you must rely exclusively on note-taking. But if you do not discover that your recorder is not working until after the interview has been completed, you are in for trouble. You will have lost all the information you received and will have wasted both your time and the other person's.

This situation happened to me once while interviewing an architect in a restaurant. Halfway through the interview, the batteries in my tape player went dead. Unfortunately, I didn't discover that fact until I attempted to listen to the tape the next day. During the interview, I had been busy eating my lunch instead of making notes, and I had no way to recall everything we had discussed. The result, as you may have guessed, was that I did not have enough information to write an article. Therefore I was required to reschedule the interview a week later and go through the same questioning again. I was lucky that the architect was able and willing to meet with me again.

Even if you trust your tape recorder and have thoroughly checked it out before you use it during the interview, you should still make a few notes during the interview. The note-taking should not be so extensive that it disrupts the flow of conversation. Rather, the notes should be short little phrases that will remind you of the answers to the questions. If the person being interviewed uses an unusual word or phrase that requires special spelling, ask for clarification and write it down.

In another instance, I conducted a long-distance interview by phone. The tape recorder I was using had a special microphone that attached to the telephone receiver so that it could record the conversation while we talked. As soon as I hung up the phone, I played back the tape and discovered that it was blank. I then found the problem: I had plugged the microphone into the headphones jack instead of the microphone jack.

Although I had never made this mistake before, I had made plenty of others in the past and had learned from them. During the conversation I had been jotting down quick notes, making an outline of what was discussed. The notes were not in complete sentences, but all the important information—dates of certain events and names of important people—was there. From these notes, I managed to reconstruct most of the conversation.

Tape recorders also pose another problem. The presence of a microphone intimidates some people. If someone is not used to a microphone, he or she may be thinking more about the tape machine than about the questions being asked. Many portable tape machines have a microphone built directly into them which minimizes this problem. Using one of these machines, the reporter simply turns on the machine and puts it in an inconspicuous place outside the subject's line of vision. Of course, the idea is not to hide the fact that you are using a tape recorder. You should always ask the person you are interviewing if you may tape the conversation and then try to help him or her become more comfortable in its presence.

In certain cases, using a tape recorder is entirely out of the question. One common example is an interview with a rock band backstage before or after a concert. Many musicians and groups do not allow recording equipment at concerts for any reason. You should always first try to get special permission from the band's manager to bring the tape recorder to the interview. If permission is denied, then you must take notes.

Camera

Some reporters bring cameras to an interview session and others work with a photographer who accompanies them to the interview. Sometimes pictures are taken at a separate session arranged by the photographer.

A camera often poses the same problem as a microphone—it can make people uneasy. Even actors and actresses, who are used to having their pictures taken, do not always like to have cameras around when they are relaxing. They may suddenly start worrying about how they look for the camera and stop concentrating on the interview questions in order to pose.

What is the best way to get a photograph of the person you are interviewing? Always complete the interview before asking if pictures can be taken. That way the person being interviewed only has to concentrate on one thing at a time. If you are taking the pictures yourself, you may want to keep your camera out of sight until it is time to use it.

If a photographer will be taking the pictures, try to arrange for him or her to arrive at the time you estimate you will be ending the interview. Or you might ask the photographer to wait outside until you have cleared the photo session with the person you are interviewing, and then have the pictures taken before the interview begins.

THE INTERVIEW

After making the appointment, doing research, preparing your questions, and gathering your equipment, finally comes the job of interviewing. While the interviewing process itself is no easy task, there are ways to make it flow smoothly.

Breaking the Ice

After you have arrived at the interview and introduced yourself to the person you will be interviewing, you should spend a couple of minutes on casual conversation before beginning the actual questioning. This kind of conversation, referred to as breaking the ice, gives both parties the opportunity to get to know one another a little before the business of the interview begins. It is a good way to get accustomed to the other person's voice and speaking habits. If you like something the person is wearing, you might want pay the person a compliment. Or, if you are interviewing someone in an office building, you may want to ask how long the company has been there. If you have read that the person enjoys sailing, you might talk about sailing for a few moments.

When I interviewed actress Carol Channing on the phone prior to her appearance in Minneapolis, I attempted to break the ice in a different way. Carol Channing is most famous for her lead role in *Hello Dolly*, the Broadway musical. Her voice, which sounds scratchy and tattered, is very distinctive and is frequently imitated by others.

The interview was scheduled to take place at a certain time, and Carol's press agent had supplied me with a phone number where she could be reached directly. When she answered the phone, I introduced myself as the writer she was expecting.

"Now Carol," I said after the introduction, "before we get started, there is something I would like to know."

"Okay, what is it," she said.

"Since I'm doing this interview over the phone and can't actually see who I am talking to, how do I really know that it's you?"

"What do you mean?" she asked.

"Well, how do I know that I'm talking to the real Carol Channing, and not talking to someone impersonating your voice?" I explained.

The voice on the other end of the line laughed. "Oh, I don't know," she said. "Have you ever heard your voice recorded?"

"Yes," I answered. "Quite often."

"And do you think it sounds like you?"

"Oh, no, not at all. I think I sound much more suave and sophisticated in real life."

"Well, you see what I mean? Whenever I hear my recorded voice, I don't think it sounds like me at all," Carol confessed. "So I don't know how I can guarantee that who you are talking to is the real Carol Channing. I guess you'll just have to take my word for it."

"Okay, I guess I will," I replied, and we both laughed.

Since Carol Channing had played a number of offbeat characters during her career, I had suspected that she would have a sense of humor and would appreciate my challenge as to who belonged to the voice on the phone. Being able to kid around a bit before commencing with the serious questions enabled us to establish a different rapport than if we had started right away with the serious stuff. From that point on, Carol treated me not so much as a stranger asking her questions but more as a friend on the other end of the phone. The result was an interview in which Carol responded candidly to the questions put to her. When I concluded the interview, Carol asked if I was planning to attend her stage performance.

"Yes, I have plans to," I answered.

"Well, Mr. D.L., I want you to come backstage

after the show and introduce yourself to me. I'd love to meet you." I thanked her and hung up.

Easing into an interview with a joke, as I did with Carol Channing, is not always the best way to start an interview. Not everyone has Carol Channing's sense of humor and not everyone would have responded to my joke the way she did. Someone else may have thought she was being made fun of, and the interview could have gotten off to a very bad start.

In each case, you must judge how to open the interview. Generally speaking, both parties involved in an interview are aware that there is a job to be done. The reporter seeks information, and the person being interviewed can supply the information. Even famous people with busy, hectic schedules know that an interview is often to their benefit. When the interview is printed, it helps to keep the person's name in front of the public. Unless you are interviewing someone under stressful circumstances, like the police chief mentioned earlier, you will probably find your interview subject extremely cooperative.

Getting Down to Business

As with all forms of conversation, an interview will have its own rhythm and flow. As the interview progresses, you will begin to notice the particular way that the other person talks. Understanding this speech pattern will help you determine when a question has been answered fully or when the other person is simply pausing to collect his or her thoughts. Because your questions have been arranged in a logical manner, the conversation should flow smoothly.

During the interview, you should always pay attention to everything that is being said. Never forget that you are engaged in an interesting conversation with another person. Certain rules of etiquette apply to the interview situation just as they apply to everyday life.

The basic rule of etiquette that all reporters follow—you probably heard it from the time you first began to speak—is *Never interrupt while someone else is speaking.* The point of an interview is to gain information from another person. If you interrupt while that person is talking, you will only hamper the interviewing process and may even cause the person to lose his or her train of thought.

If someone strays too far from your original question without answering it, you must try to direct the conversation back to the question. You can either restate the question, gently reminding the person that the discussion has veered from the subject. Or you can rephrase the question in a different way.

In some cases, you may realize that the new topic of conversation is one you hadn't thought of and is providing worthwhile information that you will be able to use. You then might want to allow the conversation to continue in that direction. In the end, you must judge each situation for yourself. The interview time is limited and you can't afford to waste too much time gathering information that you know you can't use in place of the information you need.

One of the biggest mistakes that young reporters frequently make during an interview is to finish a sentence for the person who is speaking or to put words into his or her mouth. The person being interviewed might pause after saying, "I first learned how to tie a square knot when I was. . ." and the reporter, anticipating the end, says, "in the Boy Scouts?" Although the person being interviewed might agree with the reporter, this may not have been what he originally intended to say. Perhaps the person was going to say, "I first learned how to tie a square knot when I was on a camping trip in Montana with the Boy Scouts." Because the reporter finished the sentence, a different meaning will have been recorded.

In asking your questions, you should always try to phrase them so that they cannot be answered with a simple yes or no. Perhaps a reporter wants to know how an actor felt about his last movie, which was a bomb. To ask, "Did you feel bad when your last movie wasn't a hit?" will probably bring a one-word answer: yes. A more productive way to pose the question might be to ask, "How did you feel when your last movie failed to be a hit?" To respond to this question, the actor will have to elaborate and the reporter will be supplied with more information.

When you do ask a question that brings a yes or no answer, you must follow up the answer with another question for clarification. You might ask, "Why do you feel that way?" or "Could you explain how you came to that decision?"

As you begin to interview people, from time to time someone will say something that will remind you of a similar situation that happened to you. In a normal conversation, you would probably relate your story. In an interview, however, you must remember that you're there to get the other person's story, not to tell your own. A good reporter does not talk about him or herself during the interview.

It is also important to keep in mind that everyone has a story to tell. No matter who you are interviewing, whether it is the President of the United States or the quarterback of the high school football team, that person has something important to say. Good reporters show the same level of respect and courtesy to all their interview subjects. Interviewing an actress who has just won an Academy Award will certainly differ from interviewing an eleven-year-old girl who has just won a 4-H ribbon, in part because the actress has more experience being interviewed. The success of your story, though, will be determined by how comprehensive your interview is. To guarantee its outcome, then, you must treat all of your interview subjects with equal importance.

When Things Go Wrong

No matter how much preparation you put into an interview, there will be times when you will encounter situations that turn into major problems. Some problems may not have good solutions. Some of the more common problems, though, can have a happy ending.

What happens if the person you are interviewing just doesn't answer your questions? In some cases the person will ignore your question completely and talk about something else. In other cases, the person will give vague answers. It is up to you to figure out whether the person doesn't want to talk about a certain subject or is simply unaware of his or her own behavior.

If you have tried to ask the same question in a variety of ways and still get no response, you should probably drop that line of questioning and move on to another topic. Ideally, the person will find the new topic more interesting and will become more talkative. You can always return to the original topic later in the interview.

Sometimes, though, the person you are talking to does not realize that his or her answers are not specific enough. Often if you ask the person to elaborate, you will get the information you need.

Unresponsive phone interviews are even more difficult to handle. Without eye contact and body language to convey your sincerity, you must rely on your tone of voice and clear enunciation to do it for you.

It may be that the person you are interviewing is not unresponsive, just distracted. He or she may feel uncomfortable in the surroundings or may be busy looking at what is going on around the two of you. I've interviewed rock stars backstage after a concert who were anxious to leave the dressing room and didn't feel like concentrating.

If you notice this kind of situation, think of an alternative way to handle it. Perhaps you can suggest a walk to a nearby coffee shop or someplace else out of the way. The same tactic can be employed if you are interviewing a business person whose office phone is constantly ringing.

Sometimes you will have no choice but to interview someone in an area full of distractions.

Because of busy schedules, a large percentage of interviews are actually conducted over lunch in restaurants or cafes. This might be the only time someone can get away from his or her office to meet with a reporter. And some people are simply more comfortable meeting a stranger over lunch or dinner.

Because of the normal activity involved with being served a meal, you should be prepared to have the conversation interrupted a couple of times during the meeting. You may even have to remind the person you are interviewing where you were before being interrupted. It is wise to wait until the food has been ordered before starting with your questions; you can use the time beforehand for casual conversation.

If you are using a tape recorder for the interview, you should ask to be seated away from the main activity of the room so the tape recorder will not pick up unnecessary noise.

AFTER THE INTERVIEW

Congratulations! You just completed your first interview and you did it successfully. Now what will you do with the information? After the interview comes the process of assimilating all the information gathered and incorporating it into an interesting story.

Transcribing Your Notes

If you have chosen to use a tape recorder during your interview, you must now **transcribe** it. In other words, you must listen to the tape and write down the conversation. Because people usually speak much faster than they write or type, the act of transcribing a tape will take twice as long as the interview itself. If you have an hour-long interview on tape, it will probably take you at least two hours to transcribe the entire tape.

The first few times you tape an interview, you will want to transcribe the entire session from hello to goodbye. That way you can be sure that you haven't missed anything important. Reviewing the interview on paper is also a good way to study your interviewing technique. Were your questions well-phrased? Did you miss any conversation cues? Did you interrupt the speaker?

As you gain experience, you will find that for some stories you will not need to transcribe the entire tape. You may not be using any of the information gained in the initial few moments of casual conversation, and you'll find that some of the other conversation won't be pertinent either. You will learn to recognize the quotes you can use from the interview to compose the story and can transcribe only these.

When you aren't using a tape recorder, you will need to rewrite your notes while the conversation is still fresh in your mind. Notes help you remember the main ideas and important facts. From sketchy notes, you should be able to reconstruct what was discussed during the interview in a fairly accurate fashion. The longer you wait after the interview before doing this, the greater the chances that you might forget something and lose valuable information. You should develop the habit of taking fifteen or twenty minutes right after the interview to write down all the details you can remember that aren't already in your notes.

Using the Information

How you use the information gained in an interview depends on what you set out to do in the first place. If it was a fact-finding interview you were on, you probably already knew how you were going to use the information. Let's return for a moment to the example of the reporter who is working on a story about a new convention center and theater, introduced in Chapter 1. While researching the story, the reporter learned that the theater was designed to seat 4,500 people and is estimated to cost 3 million dollars. The reporter, however, didn't know if this information was correct, so he called Martha Lee on the planning committee. Ms. Lee told the reporter, "Yes, that is correct. We plan to have the project completed in two years."

When the reporter writes the story, he can use a **direct quote** or simply **attribute** the facts to the person who said them. To illustrate this, let's look at how the article might read.

The city planning committee announced today its proposal for the new Arts Theater, to be constructed in downtown Summerville. Once completed, the $3 million theater will be able to accommodate 4,500 people, committee members say.

"We plan to have the project completed in two years," member Martha Lee said about the completion date.

Since the authority on the subject is the committee member and not the reporter, in the first paragraph the reporter attributed the information to the representative from the planning committee, who knew the projected costs and seating facilities. The information used is not in quotation marks because Martha Lee did not actually say that it would cost $3 million and hold 4,500 people. Lee said "Yes, that is correct" when the reporter inquired about the facts.

In the second paragraph, the reporter used a direct quote from Martha Lee to tell the readers when the theater would be finished. The words used in the direct quote are the exact words of the person who was interviewed.

It is very important that a reporter or writer does not **misquote** a person, or change his or her words, when writing an article. If a writer decides to use a quote in the article, it must be written *exactly* as the person spoke the sentence. If the sentence isn't used exactly as it was spoken, then it is attributed to the person who said it and does not appear in quotation marks.

The following three paragraphs illustrate the options a reporter can use between a direct quote

and an attribution. The sample is taken from an
interview I conducted with a comedian who lives
and works in Minneapolis.

> Things are going so well for this funny man
> that he has now encountered the road sign many
> of our local comics eventually pass: "Go to L.A."
> Hansen, the good Midwestern boy that he is, is
> very pragmatic about his choices and has opted
> to do "shuttle comedy." That is, he lives in
> Minneapolis and travels to California for two to
> four weeks at a time to try his luck.
>   "There is no way you can make money out
> there for quite a while," he maintains. "Even
> people who go out there still have to come back
> here to make money to support themselves."
>   The good money is made touring the clubs in
> the landlocked states, not hashing it out for
> a "maybe" spot on David Letterman's show,
> Hansen says.

The first paragraph prepares the reader for the
information I wanted to communicate, that the
comic has decided to stay in his hometown to live.
The second paragraph uses a direct quote that
explains why the comic has chosen the lifestyle
he has. The third paragraph uses information the
comic told me during the interview, but it isn't
word-for-word as the man said it during our conversation. Because it is his idea but it has been

reworded, I tell the reader where the information came from, attributing it to the comic by writing "Hansen says" at the end of the sentence.

There will be other times when a reporter chooses to write the article using the interview **verbatim**. In this kind of article, the interview is printed exactly, word-for-word, as it happened. This format is used most often when interviewing a very famous person with whom most readers are already familiar. When using this format, the reporter might choose to write a brief introductory paragraph about the person he or she interviewed. The interview is then printed with both the questions and the answers written out. Here is how the Evander Holyfield interview shown on "The Arsenio Hall Show" would look written in verbatim style.

Q: Why does your mom call you Chubby?
A: It's something that I've asked her, because I was short, but I wasn't fat—she named me after her girlfriend.
Q: Really?
A: Well, it wasn't too cool, but it stuck with me.
Q: And she still calls you Chubby?
A: I'm still her little baby!
Q: You're still real close to your mom, aren't you?
A: She's my inspiration. . . .

Often, instead of using Q and A to show who is speaking, the writer will use the initials of the people or the magazine. Here we've used the initials of the people speaking.

> AH: You're still real close to your mom, aren't
>   you?
> EH: She's my inspiration....

Writing the interview verbatim, or exactly as it was spoken, is called a **question-and-answer interview**. In this type of article, biographical and historical details are not brought into the written piece, although they are sometimes used in an introductory section. While this does not give a very broad picture of an interview, it is quite effective in cases where what the person *says* is more important than who the person *is*.

News briefings by politicians are often printed in this manner because it is important to let the words stand by themselves without interpretation from the reporter. Don't forget, though, that you must also write your questions exactly as you asked them. If you think you will be writing an interview in question-and-answer form, it is particularly important to have thought out your questions and to phrase them well.

Knowing which style best suits your subject

will take some practice, and you may find yourself writing up the same interview in more than one style to see which works best. Fairly soon, though, a style should begin to suggest itself each time you plan an interview.

It is likely that you will choose the **narrative** style most frequently, since it is much easier for readers to follow. A narrative article reads like a story and contains a beginning, a middle, and an end. Facts and details about the subject are interspersed with quotes. Both the article on the new convention center, page 48, and the interview with the comic, page 50, were written in the narrative style. The narrative style enables the reporter to use facts gained from research as well as the information obtained from the interview.

In the narrative style, the reader is also able to benefit from the reporter's observations, which would have to be left out of a question-and-answer interview. In the Evander Holyfield example printed earlier, the reader has no idea what Evander Holyfield was wearing during the interview, where it took place, or what information the reporter's research uncovered. In a narrative article, all this information could be used to give the reader a broader picture of the subject.

A long narrative article about someone in particular is often referred to as a **personality profile**.

One of the purposes of a personality profile is to give the reader some insight into the character and personality of the person being interviewed. The reporter does not want to rely solely on the information gained in the interview, but adds information from many other sources. Very often other individuals are asked to comment on the person, and their quotes are used.

Whichever method you use for writing your interview, keep in mind that an article is not simply a report. Although it gives facts, your written piece must also be interesting enough to keep the reader's attention. Your purpose as a reporter and a writer is to present the interview in a manner that gives as complete a picture as possible.

Post-Interview Follow-Up

As you are writing your article, you may find that you are missing an important piece of information. It may be that you didn't ask the question during the interview or that the person you interviewed didn't answer it adequately. Or perhaps you suddenly realize that you don't understand the answer and have no idea what the other person intended to say. In situations like these, you will want to follow up, or get back in touch with the person you interviewed to get more information or straighten out the meaning of what you have.

In some cases, this will not be possible. If your interview was with someone who was just in town for a few days, you may not be able to reach that person in time to complete your article. When that happens, you will have to write your article without using that information. You should *never* use information you are unsure of.

In those cases where you can reach the person, you'll probably have little trouble handling the matter over the phone. After all, your interview subject is just as eager as you are to make sure that all of the information printed about him or her is correct.

Keeping Your Notes

Always keep the notes and transcriptions of your interviews, even after your article has been published. If you should be questioned later, you can review your notes to reply to the question. And if you are accused of making a factual error in an article, you can return to the notes to see where you got your information.

To illustrate one kind of problem that can arise after an article is printed, let's imagine that a reporter, Randy Adams, is interviewing Angela Gomez, who organized a neighborhood council to see that all dogs are kept on leashes. During the interview, Mrs. Gomez tells the reporter that the reason she wants dogs kept on leashes is that her son has been bitten by dogs twice, one time requiring hospitalization. Mrs. Gomez believes that loose dogs are a menace to the children of the neighborhood.

In the news story, the reporter explains why the neighborhood council was established. He uses the information he gathered from Mrs. Gomez as background material, stating that Mrs. Gomez, one of the council members, believes that stray dogs are a menace because her son has been bitten twice by dogs.

After the story is printed, Mrs. Gomez calls the reporter and says that she was misquoted in the article. That is, the facts that the reporter wrote about Mrs. Gomez were not true. Mrs. Gomez says that her son wasn't bitten twice by dogs, but that he was only scared to walk to school because of the dogs in the neighborhood.

If the reporter has kept his notes from the interview, he can review them and find the reason for the discrepancy. Perhaps the reporter mis-understood Mrs. Gomez. She may have said that her son *could* have been bitten two times. Or she may have said that her *neighbor's* son had been bitten twice and went to the hospital once. Another possibility, of course, is that Mrs. Gomez has changed her story. But unless he has kept his notes, Randy can only rely on his memory. If he does have his notes or a tape of the conversation, he can review them carefully and see where the problem occurred.

Misquoting someone can be a serious issue for a reporter and the news source—newspaper, magazine, TV or radio station—the reporter works for. If the person being misquoted feels that the reporter purposely changed the information and used it to make her or him look bad, the person may decide to sue the reporter and the news source for **libel**.

Libel can be defined as a statement, knowingly spoken or printed, so erroneous that it damages the reputation of the person about whom it is said. A libelous statement can be one that is completely false, or one that may be true in one situation but not when used **out of context**.

To understand how statements can be taken out of context, let's imagine that you are standing in the hallway at school, talking with your friend Mary. The two of you are discussing a school play in which another friend, Tim, had the lead role. Mary says to you, "I didn't like Tim in the play because he didn't seem very realistic. He made me nervous because he just didn't seem to have any idea what was going on." Someone passing by overhears your conversation and heads straight to Tim with the news. But instead of repeating that Mary didn't like Tim's performance in the play, the person says, "Mary doesn't like being around you because you have no idea what's going on."

The information being passed on is fairly accurate, except for one crucial difference. Mary was talking about Tim in the context of the school play, not in the context of his everyday life.

Sometimes statements taken out of context simply make someone look foolish; at other times they actually damage his or her reputation. It is in the latter case that someone might have grounds to bring a libel suit against the reporter or the publication that printed the information.

In a libel case, the reporter's only defense is the original tape, the transcription, or the notes from the interview. It is wise to keep all of this material on hand even after the article has been printed.

Saying Thanks

As a courtesy to the person you interviewed, you should always send him or her a copy of the printed article. Almost everyone, even people who are constantly in the limelight, like to read what is written about them. When you have scheduled an interview through a press agent, you will also want to send the press agent a copy of the published article. That way, you can begin to establish a good working relationship with the press agent. Most press agents represent more than one person, and you never know when you will have the occasion to work with that person again. It will help if he or she remembers your name and your work.

IT'S YOUR TURN!

Throughout this book I have given you hints on how to interview someone with an end toward writing about it. Although many **broadcast journalists**—radio and television personalities—have similar interviewing skills, the professionals discussed in this book have been **print journalists**, the people who make their living writing for newspapers and magazines. In either case, the methods of interviewing remain the same; it's only the final product that differs.

Where to Begin

Perfecting good interviewing skills is not a trait a reporter learns in a short time. Just as a dancer or football player starts practicing at an early age, the person who is serious about studying writing and reporting begins to study the process of interviewing early. One does not need to be a reporter for a city newspaper to begin interviewing. There are also a number of opportunities for a junior high school student to practice interviewing techniques.

As a matter of fact, most of you have probably already interviewed someone without even knowing it. For instance, perhaps your grandparents recently took a vacation to Mexico or Europe. When they returned you talked to them about their trip. "Did you see any castles?" you might have asked. "What was the food like?" "How do people dress over there?"

Asking specific questions about a subject you yourself know little of is exactly what interviewing is all about. The only real difference between your line of questioning and a reporter's is that you probably were not taking notes for an article. The outstanding characteristic of a successful interviewer is a curious nature. Curiosity is the same whether you are asking a friend about a recent trip or asking a movie star about a recent movie. If you are interested in interviewing other people, there are a number of places to begin.

School Reports

Everyone is required to write a school report at one time or another, particularly in history or English class. Most of the time the information used in school reports comes from library research, but there is no reason some of it can't also be obtained by interviewing people.

In history, for example, you might be required to write a report on Brazil. You could get the majority of your material from an encyclopedia, but you should also ask around. Maybe you know someone who recently visited the country or whose grandmother was born in Brazil. You could ask that person a few questions.

Perhaps you are required to write a report on violins for music class. You might try to find a shop where violins are made. Talk to the people who work there and find out what skills and tools are required to make the instrument. Whenever you are assigned a topic to research, find out if there is someone who is an authority on the subject whom you can interview.

School Newspaper

Most junior high and high schools have a school newspaper. This is an excellent place for the young interviewer to start learning the craft.

With any school newspaper, there would be ample opportunities to interview people. When the football team wins a game, interview the star player and the coach to get their reactions to winning. If a classmate puts together an unusual science project, interview her or him and write up the information as a personality profile. You might want to ask questions about where the idea for the science project came from, how long it took to complete, and whether the person has any more projects in mind.

Interview the cheerleaders when they are elected to the squad to find out if any of them studied dance or gymnastics before tryouts. You may even find out that the school principal has an unusual hobby like skin diving or quilting; a story like this would make an excellent interview.

Practice for Celebrity Interviews

The chances are that you won't have an opportunity to interview someone *really* famous for several years, and then probably only when you represent a newspaper or magazine. But you can practice now for Luke Perry and Julia Roberts by interviewing public figures in your own town or city.

There are, of course, varying degrees of fame, and there is no reason to assume that you have to start out interviewing Michael Jackson or Madonna. People are famous for different reasons —one might be a singer, a local TV personality, or the youngest person to have climbed to the top of Mount McKinley. Look around you; in your community you will find many people who are famous for one reason or another.

Unless you live in a very large city you will probably find your mayor willing to grant you an interview. An article printed in a high school paper may bring the mayor more goodwill than an article printed in the city paper.

Try calling up one of your local TV or radio announcers with a request for an interview. If one turns you down, try another. What you learn about the newscaster's job will make a fascinating personality profile and may even help you decide if you want to pursue a career in journalism.

The more practice you get interviewing, the more confidence you will have. You will reach the point where you will no longer be intimidated by people more powerful or well-known than you. *Then* you're ready for Luke and Julia!

Career Opportunities

Professional newspaper and TV reporters are not the only people whose jobs require sharp interviewing skills. The press agents who work for singers, actors, and actresses have to know how to interview. Press agents often write **press releases**, or short articles, about their clients. They send press releases to newspapers and magazines. They must know how to get the proper information from the people they represent.

Outside the realm of the **media**, or newspapers, magazines, TV, and radio, there are many other job possibilities that require interviewing skills. All large corporations, like IBM or General Mills, have public relations departments. The function of a public relations department is to create a degree of understanding between the company and the public. Public relations people do this by explaining the corporation's policies and activities to people outside of the company.

Other Rewards

Almost any time you look for a job, at some point you will go to a job interview where *you* will be interviewed. The person who is considering hiring you for a job asks you questions about yourself and your background, trying to determine who, of all the people applying for the job, is most qualified to fill the position. If you know how to conduct a good interview, you will be more relaxed when someone is interviewing you. You should also take the opportunity to interview the employer and find out more about the job and the company.

So even if you are not considering a career as a journalist, press agent, public relations person, or in some media-related field, firsthand knowledge of the interviewing process just might land you the job you *do* want.

And there's an even greater benefit from developing good interviewing skills. Good interviewers are good listeners because they have learned to hear what others are saying, instead of concentrating only on their own thoughts. As your interviewing skills increase, you'll find that your powers of observation are increasing too. You may even find that you understand your friends and family a little better than you did before.

GLOSSARY OF TERMS

attribute: to identify the source of information within a written article or to credit the speaker

body language: the gestures and mannerisms with which a person communicates his or her thoughts and feelings

direct quote: the actual words spoken or written by a person

fact-finding interview: an interview conducted to obtain specific facts or the answers to specific questions

informational interview: an interview conducted to obtain general knowledge about a person, subject, or event

interview: a meeting, either in person or by telephone, at which one person obtains information from another

journalist: a person who collects information and edits or writes it for presentation to the public. A **broadcast journalist** is a journalist whose work appears on TV or radio, while the work of a **print journalist** appears in newspapers or magazines.

libel: a written or spoken statement or representation that is false or that unjustly conveys an unfavorable impression

media (plural of **medium**): the channels of communication for news and entertainment, taken as a whole, including newspapers, radio, and television

misquote: to quote incorrectly, either adding, omitting, or changing words so that they are not quoted exactly as spoken or written

narrative: an article written in story form

out of context: removed from the surrounding background, or context, so that the meaning is altered

personality profile: an article that focuses on an individual person, offering special insight into that person's life, history, or work

press agent: a person employed to establish and maintain good relations with journalists in order to encourage and control publicity

press release: a written report about the newsworthy activities of an individual or organization designed to inform the public

public relations: an office or a department whose function is to explain the policies and activities of an individual or organization to the general public for the purpose of promoting understanding and goodwill

question-and-answer interview: a format for writing an interview in which both the questions and the answers are written word for word and no additional commentary is included

transcribe: to transfer information from a tape recorder to the written page by listening to the tape and writing or typing the words

verbatim: word for word

ABOUT THE AUTHOR

D.L. Mabery's curiosity led him into journalism when he was attending Utah State University. He earned a degree in journalism and, after a short stint of work in Los Angeles, moved to Minneapolis, Minnesota. Mr. Mabery has conducted hundreds of interviews, from comedians to musical groups to political figures, and is currently the arts and entertainment editor of a weekly newspaper.